This book is presented to

_____

from

_____

Thank you to five loving angels
Victoria, Amie, Jill, Adele, and Mary.
You are my inspiration.

DO YOU WONDER WHO GOD IS?

Written and Illustrated by
Laura N. Bourree

GOD is the warmth of the sun.

GOD is
the light of
the moon...

and the twinkle
of the stars.

GOD is
the raindrop you can taste on your tongue.

He is
the hug of a
lonely friend.

GOD is
the waves on the ocean,
the rush of the river,
and the calm on the lake.

GOD is
the scent of a
beautiful flower.

GOD is
the buzz of a bee,
the purr of a kitten,
and the roar of a lion.

GOD is
the sweetness
of a mother's kiss.

GOD is
the sound of silence,
the keeper of time,
the ultimate weaver...

and the master of eternity.

GOD is
the feeling of peace.

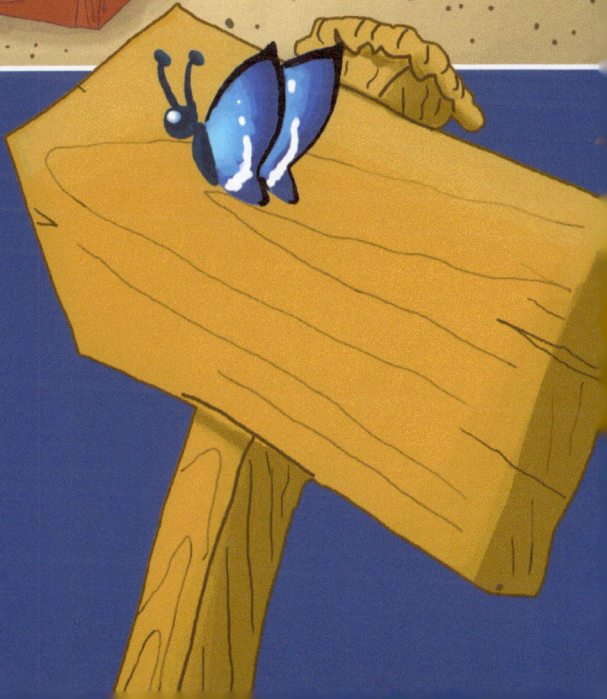

GOD is joy.

GOD is love.

GOD is
and will always be your very best friend.

JESUS + JILL WERE HERE

GOD is
one with
many names.

KINGDOM OF GOD

GOD is
your father,
your mother...

and your teacher.

And Jesus said, "Let the little children come to me, and do not hinder them, for the Kingdom of God belongs to them."

And Jesus said, "The Lord our God is one Lord." "Love the Lord thy God with all thy heart, and with all thy soul, and with all thy mind, and with all thy strength."

GOD is
your destiny.

GOD is
your hope and
dreams come true.

GOD is
the light that
guides your way.

GOD is
in everything
he has created.

Insert child's photo here

ESPECIALLY YOU!

Give me, give me, give me God

~ A child's prayer ~

Give me the mind to make good choices.

Give me the eyes to see your beauty.

Give me the ears to hear your guidance.

Give me the mouth to speak the truth.

Give me the heart to feel compassion.

Give me the arms to embrace your love.

Give me the hands to help others.

Give me the feet to walk in your direction.

Amen

You are a child of God.
Dream beautiful dreams and
know that God loves you.
God is with you always.

Child's affirmation

I am God's precious child.

I respect all people, animals, and living creatures of every kind.

For God is in all of these.

I care for the lands, mountains, and seas.

For God has provided these.

I love God with all my mind, heart, and soul.

For the heavens of God were made for me.